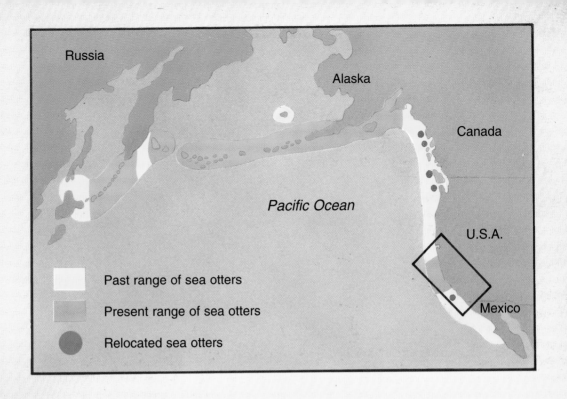

Russia

Alaska

Canada

Pacific Ocean

U.S.A.

Mexico

▢ Past range of sea otters

▢ Present range of sea otters

● Relocated sea otters

P9-ELR-855

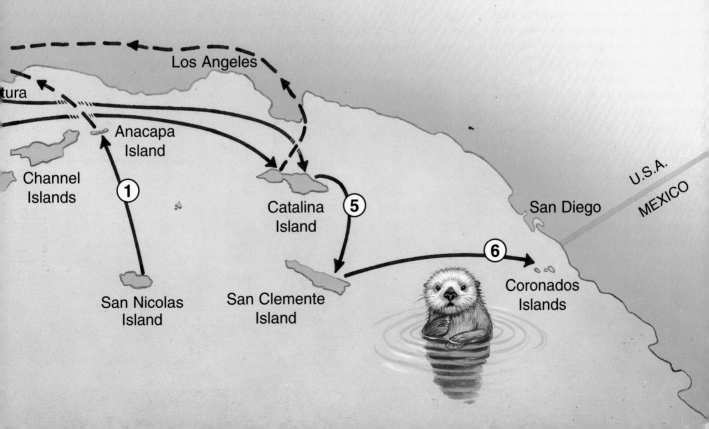

Los Angeles

tura

Anacapa
Island

Channel
Islands

①

Catalina
Island

⑤

San Diego

U.S.A.

MEXICO

⑥

Coronados
Islands

San Nicolas
Island

San Clemente
Island

THE ADVENTURES OF PHOKEY THE SEA OTTER

BASED ON A TRUE STORY

By Marianne Riedman, Ph.D.
Illustrated by Paul Lopez

△ SEQUOYAH PUBLISHING

The Woods Publishing Group

Published by
Sequoyah Publishing
P. O. Box 1415
Capitola, California 95010

In association with
The Woods Publishing Group
San Diego, California

© 1996 by Sequoyah Publishing
Text Copyright © 1996 by Marianne Riedman
All rights reserved. No part of this book may be reproduced or utilized
in any form or by any means, electronic or mechanical, including photocopying,
recording, or by any information storage and retrieval system,
without permission in writing from the publisher.

Printed in Hong Kong through Global Interprint, Petaluma, California
Designed by The Woods Publishing Group
First Edition
2 3 4 5 6 7 8 9 10

Library of Congress Catalog Card Number: 95-71194

Publisher's Cataloging in Publication
(Prepared by Quality Books Inc.)
Riedman, Marianne
The adventures of Phokey the sea otter: based on a true story/
by Marianne Riedman; illustrated by Paul Lopez. p. cm.
Summary: The story of a young sea otter released at an island off
southern California, his many adventures with the island seals and sea lions,
and his amazing long-distance journeys along the coast.
Includes a Fun Facts section about sea otters.

ISBN 0-9648600-0-7
1. Sea otters—Juvenile Literature.   I. Title.
QL737.C25R54 1996   599.74'447

Photo Credits: Fun Facts photographs by Marianne Riedman
Back cover photograph by Chris Angelos; Jacket flap photograph by Michelle Staedler

For my grandfather
— M.L.R

AUTHOR'S NOTE

This book is based on a true story about a California sea otter that was named Phokey (pronounced Fō´-kēy) because he loved to play with harbor seals, whose scientific name is *Phoca vitulina*. The facts about sea otters (*Enhydra lutris*) and other marine animals presented in this story are accurate and based on current scientific research.

Acknowledgments—Special thanks to David Dawson for designing the book and Walter Stuart for the map illustration, Linda Wood, Darrel Millsap, Emahó, and my family, especially my grandfather, mother, and father. Thanks also to Brian Hatfield, Greg Sanders, and other biologists from the U.S. Fish & Wildlife Service and California Department of Fish & Game, and to Campbell Grant for permission to include rock art symbols from *The Rock Paintings of the Chumash*.

1

An Otter Pup Loses His Mother

One day, as the warm October sun was rising over Monterey Bay, a tiny sea otter pup was born. His mother took good care of him. She nursed him with her creamy, rich milk. She groomed his silky fur and kept it clean and fluffy. And she shared her food with him.

This mother otter especially liked to eat crabs. Like other California sea otters, she was a choosy eater. Each of her otter neighbors also ate only one or two kinds of food. One liked clams and octopuses. Another ate only snails. The pup was learning to be a crab-eater, like his mother.

The pup grew fat on crabs and milk, and the days passed peacefully until one cold January morning when a fierce winter storm churned up the ocean. Rain poured down on the mother otter and her baby until they were soaked. Icy winds swept along the shore and drowned out their cries. Snuggling deeper into his mother's warm belly, the pup clung to her soft fur. Suddenly, a huge wave tore the baby otter away from his mother.

Tossed and tumbled in the foamy seas, the pup cried and cried for his mother. But she was gone. Now he was on his own. Even though the young otter was nearly four months old, he was not quite ready to be weaned.

When the skies were blue and the sun was shining again, the orphaned pup searched for his mother. But he couldn't find her anywhere. Exhausted by the storm, the pup crawled onto a beach and curled up in the warm sand. He was cold and hungry, and he began to whimper softly.

After a while, the orphan found that he was surrounded by a circle of people. Someone had noticed the tiny otter and had called the wildlife rescue team. Now he was in their hands. They would have to take over where his mother had left off, since she was nowhere to be seen.

The pup was too weak to resist when someone scooped him up and whisked him into a waiting car. The rescuers took the frightened baby otter to a special sea mammal rescue center where he could be cared for until he was strong enough to survive on his own.

Everyone looked worried as they watched the thin and shivering bundle of fur.

"Oh, I hope he'll live!" whispered one of the rescuers.

2

A Trip to San Nicolas Island

In his strange new home, the otter pup was afraid of people and hissed if they came too close. But he hungrily gulped down the food that his human caretakers placed in his tank, especially the crabs.

For three months the pup rested and ate. Gradually he grew strong again, and people didn't seem to scare him so much. At last, he was ready to be released back into his ocean home. No one knew it yet, but he would not be like the other otters, and he was to have many strange adventures that would earn him the nickname "Phokey."

One day some marine biologists came to visit Phokey. It was their job to watch over him once he was released back into the wild. They looked down at the big pup resting in his outdoor tank. He opened one sleepy eye and watched them as they talked softly about where to set him free.

They could release him where most of the other sea otters lived along the central California coast. Or they could let him go at San Nicolas Island, far to the south of where the other otters lived. A small group of California otters had been moved to this island to protect them in case there was an oil spill in their mainland home.

Finally, they decided to give him a new home at San Nicolas Island. The island waters were rich with otter food, and the biologists thought the pup would have an easier time surviving on his own there. They hoped he would be happy at the island.

So one morning in May, Phokey found himself flying in an airplane that was heading to his new island home. He nibbled at the lime green and white tags that the biologists had placed on his flippers so he would be easy to spot. One tag was really a tiny radio. It would send signals for a few weeks, which would help the biologists track the young otter to make sure he was all right.

After many hours of being jostled about, Phokey could finally hear the sound of breaking waves and smell the salty ocean air. He paced anxiously in his cage.

At last the biologists set the cage on the beach and opened the door. He was free! Phokey bounded into the surf, pausing once to glance back at the people on the beach. They took one long, last look at the pup through their binoculars. Then he swam out to sea and vanished.

For many days the biologists searched for their otter. But they couldn't find him. They listened for his radio signal from a plane that flew all along the California coast, but they could hear nothing. Feeling very sad that he might have perished, they went home.

3

The Anacapa Island Otter

Two years passed. There had been no sign of the lost otter, and everyone had forgotten about him. Then one spring day, an old Chumash Indian was tending his lobster traps at an island called Anacapa, almost 60 miles from San Nicolas Island. His young granddaughter was with him. They noticed a furry brown creature looking curiously at them from the water. It looked like a stuffed animal that had come alive.

The fisherman looked puzzled. It wasn't a harbor seal. It wasn't a sea lion.

"It's a ... *sea otter!*" whispered the fisherman to his granddaughter in an excited voice. A piece of white tag flashed on its flippers. Phokey was alive! And he had grown into a healthy three-year-old. His thick and glossy fur coat had already started to turn golden-white around his cheeks and forehead.

"But, Grandfather, you said that no sea otters have lived here for 100 years!"

"Yes, that's true." Once thousands of otters had flourished on all of

the southern California islands. But they were hunted almost to extinction for their lush and beautiful fur.

"I don't understand how, but a sea otter has made its way back to the islands," said the grandfather. "He has found his ancient home."

Phokey could hear their voices and rose up out of the water to get a better view of the old man and the girl with shining black hair. He stretched his neck far up into the air until he looked like a submarine periscope.

"Won't he be lonely?" asked the girl. "No other otters are here. Will he be all right?"

"I don't know, little one. I hope so. But there are many dangers in the sea for a young animal like this, especially one so . . . curious."

Near the otter the water was bubbling. He swam over to the foaming bubbles and sniffed. They had a human smell. Following the bubbles to the bottom, Phokey found two scuba divers who were busy looking at something underneath a rock. They wore black rubber suits from head to toe. Big metal tanks sat on their backs, and silvery air bubbles rose to the surface every time they breathed.

Phokey had a little game he liked to play with the island divers. He snuck up behind them, patted their round black heads with his paws, then sped away. This scary surprise always caused a big reaction as the startled divers whipped around and anxiously looked about. Phokey seemed to enjoy this reaction very much.

The Chumash fisherman and his granddaughter smiled. They could see the otter playing with the divers.

"You know," said the grandfather, "in old times, our people had great respect for the otter. They believed the otter's spirit was joyful, curious, and adventuresome. And most of all, playful." It was good to see a sea otter at Anacapa once again.

4

Playing with the Harbor Seals

A few days later, the girl and her grandfather saw the otter again.

"Look, Grandfather, he thinks he's a seal!" Phokey was perched on a rock, trying to blend in with a group of harbor seals. He kept patting the seals and nuzzling their faces. One black-spotted silver seal nuzzled Phokey back. But the other seals continued to bask in the warm spring sunshine, ignoring the playful otter.

Phokey made loud whining sounds. He climbed on top of one of the seals and clung to its back. The squirming seal tried to buck him off, but the little otter held on tight. Wriggling across the rock, the seal jumped into the water with Phokey still glued to its back.

"Look! He's riding the seal!" exclaimed the girl.

Rolling and somersaulting in the water, the seal and otter played together. Phokey wrapped his paws around the seal's neck. Faster and faster they spun in the water. Finally, the seal had enough. It twisted free and swam back to its resting rock. Phokey raced after it.

The girl and her grandfather laughed with delight. They'd never heard of a sea otter who liked seals so much.

"Maybe he won't be so lonely after all," said the girl.

"Maybe not..." The old fisherman smiled. "You know, our island ancestors had many legends about the otter and the seal." The grandfather loved to tell these old stories, and his granddaughter had heard them often.

"Now we have a story about a sea otter too," said the girl.

Phokey would not leave the harbor seals alone. He scrambled onto a slippery tidal rock and skidded into two seals. They toppled into the water. The otter lunged after them. Underwater he chased after the spotted silver seal and grabbed its tail. Gliding through the sunlit forest of kelp, the two played "tag" until Phokey had to streak to the surface for a breath of air.

"Look! There he is!" called the girl. "Can we come back and look for the otter again? To see if he's okay? He could get caught underwater in one of your lobster traps."

"After we check my traps at the other islands...then we'll come back," replied the grandfather, as they watched the otter chasing seals into the distance across the sparkling sea.

5

Searching for Phokey

The marine biologists finally heard some rumors that there was a sea otter at Anacapa Island, playing with the seals and teasing scuba divers.

"But that's impossible!" said one of the surprised biologists. "No sea otters live at Anacapa. Besides, otters don't play with seals and divers. They're too shy." But they decided to go to the island and see for themselves.

Later that week, three biologists made the trip to Anacapa. Inside their boat were nets, wet suits, and a small cage. Circling the island, they searched for a sea otter.

The Chumash girl was tide pooling, wading in the clear rocky pools. She saw Phokey peeking out from a dark sea cave, watching the boat. He sniffed the air warily. The girl saw the nets and asked the biologists what they were doing.

"If there's a sea otter here, we have to catch it," explained a man with windblown gray hair and a weathered face.

"Why?" asked the girl.

"Because it's the law."

"What law?"

"The law that says that otters moved to San Nicolas Island have to stay there. If any of them wander away, they have to be caught and moved back north to their home in central California. You see, many people who fish these waters are afraid that sea otters will eat too many shellfish, like sea urchins, lobster, and abalone — the same foods the fishermen depend on to make a living."

"But the otter doesn't know he's breaking the law," said the girl.

"We know ..." sighed a female biologist with binoculars. "But we still have to catch him."

From inside his sea cave Phokey spotted some harbor seals sleeping on a nearby rock. He couldn't resist. The otter made a beeline for the seals and pounced on them. They snorted loudly with surprise. One joined Phokey in the water and they wrestled playfully.

"There's the otter!" called the woman.

For many hours the biologists watched Phokey playing with the seals. They waited and waited for the otter to settle down so they could catch him. Never had they known of a sea otter that liked seals so much.

"Doesn't he ever get tired?" said one biologist, yawning.

"Maybe he thinks he's a seal instead of an otter," mused another. "After all, he never had a chance to grow up with other otters. And sea otters are social. They don't like to be alone for long. With no other otters to play with, the seals are the only companions he has."

"Let's name him *Phokey*..." suggested the woman. They all decided this was a good name, since the odd little otter so loved the harbor seals, whose scientific name is *Phoca*.

The biologists still didn't know that Phokey was the same pup that had mysteriously disappeared from San Nicolas Island. They'd have to read the broken tag hidden under his flipper to discover who he was.

Although Phokey was still busy playing with the seals, he kept an eye on the biologists in the boat as they put on their wet suits and diving gear. He watched them slip into the water with a special otter trap they had made.

Then they were gone. It was quiet, but the otter sensed that something was about to happen. Something new.

All of a sudden, Phokey felt the water currents swirling beneath him. Sticking his head underwater, he saw the divers below with a strange-looking net attached to a long pole. The otter waited on the surface until the last minute, then sprang away just as the trap was about to snap shut. A new game!

It was getting late, so the biologists decided to leave and come back another time. Hidden under a blanket of kelp fronds, Phokey kept as still as he could and watched as the boat sped away from the island.

6

Exploring the Sea Lion Beach

A few days later the biologists were back. They noticed some sea lions barking loudly and stampeding into the water. Soon the cause of the commotion came wandering through the crowded colony. Phokey! The nervous sea lions kept moving aside to make a wide path for the strange intruder. Now and then the playful otter bounded after

some of the sea lions as they rushed to the water, but they were fast swimmers and easily escaped. Finally, Phokey plopped down on the warm sand for a rest.

The biologists watched with astonished faces. This sea otter was friendly with both harbor seals *and* sea lions. But most of the sea lions were a little afraid of the otter, even though he was so much smaller than they were.

Phokey was still resting on the shore. Two of the biologists took a large net and tiptoed down the beach toward the otter. But he heard their crunchy footsteps in the sand and bounded away into the water.

The hot and tired biologists watched Phokey cooling off in the waves. It didn't look as if they would be catching him this day. So they gave up and went home, empty-handed again.

Later that day as Phokey was exploring the beach, he saw something lying on the shore and bounded toward it. Suddenly the otter stopped in his tracks. This was no sea lion. A person was curled up in the soft sand. She was like the people who had tried to catch him, but smaller. Long, dark hair held with a shiny metal clip hung down from her head.

It was the fisherman's granddaughter. She'd been watching the biologists try to catch the otter and had fallen asleep after they'd left. Phokey approached cautiously. He nuzzled her hair in the same way he nosed the seals when greeting them. The silver thing sparkled in the sun and he nibbled at it curiously.

Suddenly the girl woke up and turned over. She was face to face with a sea otter! For an instant Phokey froze, as he looked into a pair of surprised brown eyes only inches away. Then the startled otter backed away and waddled toward the water. Blinking in the bright sunlight, the girl sat up and watched him go. Her eyes were wide with wonder, and she was smiling.

Phokey's instincts told him to run from the humans on land, where otters were slow and awkward. But somehow he didn't feel afraid of the young girl anymore, for he sensed that she was kind and meant him no harm. He heard her speaking and stopped, watching her curiously.

"Poor otter. You've had two scares on the beach. First those biologists. And now me. You're so curious. I hope it doesn't get you into trouble some day. Don't be too curious about those lobster traps under the water. You could get stuck."

The otter wasn't listening anymore. He'd spotted some seals and was heading toward them. The girl watched him leave. She would not chase him, for they were now friends, and she respected the animals of the sea.

7

Phokey Causes Pandemonium

A few weeks later the biologists were back at Anacapa. This was their tenth trip to catch Phokey.

"Oh please...don't let him take that shortcut again today," mumbled one of the biologists to no one in particular.

During high tide, Phokey had a habit of swimming over the island isthmus, a thin strip of land connecting the eastern and middle parts of Anacapa Island. An otter could easily squeeze through. But the water was much too shallow for a boat. The biologists could only watch helplessly as Phokey slipped away. To catch up with him, they'd have to circle all the way around to the other side of the island.

"There he is!" someone called. They watched as Phokey crawled onto the beach and waddled into a group of sea lions and northern elephant seals. A gigantic elephant seal bull was lumbering toward the water. The otter was directly in his path.

"Uh oh! Phokey's in trouble..." said one of the biologists. The elephant seal stopped and stared nervously at the strange furry creature. It sniffed the air with its long, droopy nose. Phokey stared back. Suddenly the bull spun around and fled.

A few moments later, Phokey spotted some sea lions resting on the beach. He bounded toward them, and they scattered into the water. A big sea lion bull soaking in a tide pool didn't see Phokey until the otter crept up behind him. The bull turned and panicked. He scrambled over the tide pool rocks and rushed out to sea. Phokey chased the bull, then returned to the tide pool and relaxed. Reaching underwater, he scooped up a crab and munched on its claw. It sounded like a crunchy carrot. All the nearby sea lions turned to look at the noisy otter.

"A new beachmaster has arrived on Anacapa, and it seems to be Phokey," said one of the biologists. Everyone laughed.

The otter saw a young sea lion gazing curiously at him from the water. This looked promising! He pounced on the sea lion and hugged it

tightly. They playfully lunged at each other's faces. Suddenly, the sea lion shook free, and a high-speed chase began. Phokey was not about to let his new playmate escape.

As they sped away, the sea lion and otter jumped high into the air like slick brown torpedos. They crashed into a large group of sea lions resting on the surface, and the water began to boil with panicky sea lions. Every so often, the biologists could see the otter leaping up in the thrashing group of animals, still chasing his young sea lion friend.

"Isn't he afraid of anything?" marveled one of the biologists. The fearless otter had just caused complete pandemonium among the Anacapa seals, disturbing hundreds in a couple of hours.

"Well, this doesn't look like the day we'll be catching Phokey," someone said, but not too regretfully.

"Maybe we should put on a seal suit," suggested someone else, as they trudged back to the boat. "Then we'd catch him."

8

Phokey Heads North

It was a calm and clear October day. The three biologists had decided to search for Phokey once again. This time they were determined to catch him. As their boat slipped through the glassy sea, the gray-haired biologist had a thinking sort of frown on his face. Here they were, well-trained and serious marine biologists, in charge of managing California sea otters. But instead, a sea otter was managing them!

"Can you believe it?" he said. "This is our *24th* trip to Anacapa to catch that otter." The other two biologists were already well aware of the score: Phokey — 24; Biologists — 0.

When they reached the island, the biologists counted 90 lobster traps set in the shallow water where Phokey usually fed. But there was no sign of the otter.

The black-haired girl was busy exploring the beach.

"Have you seen an otter around here?" called one of the biologists hopefully.

"An otter? What otter? Oh, that otter. Haven't seen him." By now, the girl knew all of Phokey's favorite hiding places, but she wasn't telling. She had grown very fond of the otter.

The biologists waved goodbye and moved on. They looked around by the harbor seal rock. Phokey wasn't there.

"Sure hope he didn't get stuck in a lobster trap," someone said. The biologists knew that, once in a while, otters trying to poach crab traps got stuck and drowned. And lobster and crab were Phokey's favorite foods, after all. Everyone looked worried.

Suddenly a loud crunching sound filled the air.

Crunch, crunch, crack, crack. Looking toward shore, they saw an otter munching on a lobster. Phokey was alive!

In an instant the quiet boat turned into a wild tangle of arms and legs as everyone scrambled to put on diving gear. Phokey calmly watched the frantic biologists as he polished off the lobster and rolled from side to side to clear his chest of scraps.

"Shhhhhh!" cautioned the gray-haired biologist. The otter was now staring suspiciously at the boat.

Phokey dove again and captured two big crabs. Grabbing some strands of surfgrass, he wrapped them around one crab like a straightjacket so it couldn't escape. Then he ate the other crab.

Crunch, crunch, crunch. Into the water the divers quickly slipped with their nets. They breathed oxygen from special tanks that didn't make noisy bubbles. Phokey looked at the boat. It was quiet now. He couldn't see the biologists anymore.

Swoosh! Suddenly Phokey found himself tangled inside a big net. He had been so busy eating the crab that he'd forgotten all about the divers in the water.

The biologists had finally caught the legendary sea otter. Yet now that they were victorious at last, they looked strangely glum. There would be no more trips to Anacapa to chase the evasive otter they had come to admire. There would be no more otter antics with seals to make them laugh.

As they read the worn numbers on the otter's broken white tag, the biologists suddenly realized that this was the very same pup they had lost so long ago.

"So *this* is who Phokey is!" exclaimed someone. Everyone was truly astonished that the lost otter was still alive. Phokey weighed 62 pounds, so they knew he'd been eating well. The biologists put bright new tags on his flippers. This would help them tell him apart from the other otters.

On the deck of the boat, Phokey huddled in a cage and looked back toward Anacapa. As the boat sped away, the island grew smaller and smaller until it was just a distant speck of land. The otter made anxious squeaking sounds. Would he ever find his way back home? When they arrived at the mainland, the biologists loaded his cage into their big van and drove up the coast to Phokey's old home in Monterey. After several hours, the otter was now more than 300 miles from Anacapa.

Just north of Monterey, the biologists stopped at a spot called Moss Landing, where many other male otters lived. They had decided to let Phokey go there. After carrying his cage to the water's edge, the biologists opened the door and watched. Phokey poked his nose out and sniffed the unfamiliar air. Then he bounded to the water and dove in with a splash.

By now it was night, and all the biologists could see of Phokey were his paddling hindflippers, leaving ripples shining in the moonlight as he swam into the dark ocean waters.

9

Exploring Monterey Bay

One day in December, a lady who liked sea otters was standing on the Santa Cruz wharf. She noticed a sea otter swimming with the sea lions. The otter swam under the sea lions. It swam over the sea lions. It rubbed against the sea lions like a cat. It tried to hug the sea lions.

"Why, this otter doesn't mind the sea lions at all," she exclaimed. "In fact, he seems to like them!" She couldn't help noticing his brightly colored tags, and told some local marine biologists about the strange otter.

The next day, the biologists walked to the end of the wharf. Two young male otters were playing together. One had green and white tags. It was Phokey! And this time he was playing with another otter!

After Phokey swam away from Moss Landing, someone had spotted him along the coast of Monterey. Like most young male animals, he liked to explore new places. But many female sea otters lived in Monterey, and this meant that big territorial male otters patrolled these waters. So Phokey had traveled north to Santa Cruz, where groups of other young male otters lived.

For hours the biologists watched the two otters wrestle in the waves. The otters shoved. They pushed. They pounced. Leaping high into the air like dolphins, they chased each other into the distance. At last, Phokey had found another otter that liked to play as much as he did.

Phokey dove and caught a big red crab. His new friend stole the delicious prize, as male otters sometimes do, and this started another round of play, which lasted until the sun sank into the ocean and the clouds turned rosy pink in the sky. And that's the last anyone saw of Phokey for many months.

10

The Long Journey South

Night had fallen, and Phokey was still swimming south. He had left Santa Cruz a few days ago. The otter felt an urge, an instinctive pull, to return home to the southern islands he knew so well.

But would he make it? Such a journey could be full of dangers for a young otter, especially one as innocent and curious as Phokey. Along the way, he might come upon great white sharks, underwater fishing nets, tempting lobster traps, or even gooey oil slicks. He would have to pass by male otters guarding their territories, and angry fishermen who shot sea otters once in a while.

But tonight the stars sparkled brightly in the clear winter sky, and a full moon lit Phokey's path with a soft, cool light. Moonlight reflected off the trail of ripples that spread out behind the otter as he paddled south.

Phokey could see that the other otters he passed were also busy. Some were grooming and socializing. A few were resting. Others were swimming and eating. Sea otters didn't sleep all night. They just kept doing what they did all day.

Phokey passed Point Sur, where his ancestors — the last 50 California sea otters — hid from hunters in the early 1900s.

He passed Morro Bay Harbor, where he found a big group of male otters splashing and playing in the pink light of dawn.

He passed the Santa Maria River. The sun was now high in the sky. After a while he saw no more otters. He had swum past the southern end of the sea otters' California home and traveled more than 200 miles — nearly the otters' entire range.

He passed Point Conception. Now he was in the "no-otter zone."

Phokey headed toward Anacapa Island, but he didn't stop there. He just kept right on going until he reached an island called Catalina. He had traveled nearly 400 miles! At Catalina there were many harbor seals and scuba divers to play with and plenty of lobster and crab to eat.

But soon word spread of the strange sea otter at Catalina. Many people visited this island to swim and dive in the warm, clear waters. No one had ever seen a sea otter here before, at least not for a century.

Before long, the biologists who had lost and then found Phokey also heard of the Catalina otter. They had an idea who it might be.

So one April afternoon they traveled to Catalina. The biologists wished that they didn't have to capture and move the otter out of the "no-otter zone." But they did. It was their job.

They searched the eastern side of the island where the otter had been seen. They looked especially carefully where they found harbor seals. Sure enough, huddled in a group of seals was an otter with green and white tags. It was Phokey!

"How did Phokey find his way to Catalina?" wondered the biologists. They knew that other otters at San Nicolas Island had traveled many miles north to reach their old homes back on the

mainland. But Phokey had swum even farther, hundreds of miles south, in the opposite direction. How otters found their way back home across the open ocean was a mystery. Someday the biologists hoped to understand it.

Phokey sniffed the air and looked up. Not that boat again! It always seemed to find him, no matter where he went.

The biologists moved downwind of the otter. They lay in wait until he was busy eating a crab, then snuck up beneath him from underwater. Whoosh! The trap snapped shut. Phokey struggled inside the tangly net, but it was no use. He was caught *again*.

Once more, the biologists took Phokey back north to Moss Landing and let him go. Once more, Phokey disappeared and swam south. His second long journey back home had begun. But would he be as lucky this time?

11

Phokey Outsmarts the Biologists

By now it was June. Two months had gone by without a trace of Phokey. Although the biologists didn't know it yet, the otter had just visited some kelp beds off Ventura, very close to their research station in southern California. But Phokey didn't stay for long. He kept swimming south. A mysterious inner "compass" seemed to guide him.

The young otter was vulnerable swimming so far out to sea. It would be hard for him to find enough to eat in the deep-water channel. But he swam on and on.

Many hours passed. Phokey glanced up and ducked as a big black bird came hurtling toward him like an arrow. It was a cormorant. Smack! The bird hit the water and dove nearly 20 feet underwater. Phokey followed. He saw the long-necked bird grab a small silver fish in its beak.

Even though the otter was weak with hunger, the urge to play was irresistible. He chased the diving bird but it sped to the surface, then flew off toward an island in the distance. The otter looked toward the land. It was Catalina Island!

After reaching the lush kelp beds of Catalina, Phokey began to dive for food. Underwater he passed many lobster traps, but left them alone

for now. Patting the bottom with his paws, he reached deep into rocks and crevices, searching for food. Ouch! He felt a sharp stinging pain in his paw.

The otter found himself eye to eye with a fierce moray eel, which had given him a warning bite. With its powerful jaws and sharp teeth, the eel ate the same foods that Phokey happened to like — lobster and crab. From now on, he would remember to be more careful when sticking his paws into dark underwater caves.

Licking his sore paw, the otter spotted some harbor seals sleeping on shore and paddled over to join them for a nap. Tomorrow there would be time to play.

12

Danger at Catalina Island

Soon news traveled back to the biologists that a sea otter was at Catalina again, playing with the seals and scuba divers.

"Oh no!" exclaimed one. "Outsmarted by Phokey again." So the biologists went to Catalina and looked around where they had last seen the otter. To their amazement, he had returned to the very same spot as before!

This morning Phokey was busy chasing harbor seals. Two of the biologists slipped into the water with their trap. They hoped to surprise the otter. Underwater they strained to see the surface. He had just been there! Suddenly the divers felt something tap them from behind. Turning around, they saw Phokey speeding away. Their plan had failed. He had surprised *them*! The waterlogged biologists decided to give up and go home.

Phokey began to dive for his dinner. Underwater he spotted two fat lobsters, but they were trapped inside a cage. Phokey pawed at the cage hopefully. Nothing happened. Grabbing a heavy rock, he pounded the trap, but the lobsters stayed safe inside. A few harbor seals glided by to see what the otter was up to.

Phokey ran out of air and rose to the surface. The seals followed. Down he dove to the lobsters again. This time he reached into a small hole just big enough for his foreleg, grabbed hold of the lobster's tail, and pulled. But something was wrong. His paw was stuck! Letting go of the lobster, Phokey tried to pull his paw out. It wouldn't budge. He was trapped! Looking up, the panicked otter could see the surface only 20 feet above him. He struggled with all his strength to free himself, but it was no use.

No sea otter can hold its breath longer than about four minutes. Phokey had only two more minutes of air left. The seals had been waiting for the otter at the surface. When he didn't return, they dove to the bottom and saw him struggling with the trap. They watched for a while. Was he playing or in trouble? Soon Phokey stopped struggling, but every so often he still jerked his paw desperately.

One of the harbor seals that had been playing with Phokey earlier suddenly launched itself toward the otter in a great burst of speed. The big seal playfully bumped into the otter and knocked over the lobster trap. Phokey's paw slipped out of the cage. He was free!

Phokey shot to the surface and gulped down deep breaths of fresh air. The seal bobbed on the surface next to him. With a playful push, he had saved the otter's life.

From that time on, whenever Phokey saw a lobster trap he swam right on by. Like all sea otters, he was a quick learner. Lobsters were still on his diet, but only if they weren't in cages!

13

San Clemente Island

A few weeks later, a harbor seal watched as Phokey swam underwater through the kelp forest, clutching a crab to his chest. Silvery air bubbles streamed from the otter's fur as he rose up to the surface. A rock was tucked into the furry pouch under his arm.

Whack, whack, whack! Phokey pounded the crab with his rock tool and stuffed the tasty meat into his mouth.

The otter looked up at the island cliffs. Three people with binoculars had been watching him for a long time. It was the biologists again. They had tracked him down after hearing about a tagged otter on San Clemente Island.

"If Phokey travels any farther south, he'll be in Mexico!" declared the female biologist.

"How did he find San Clemente Island?" asked one of the others. The island is almost 60 miles south of Catalina. But they all knew that no one had the answer, except perhaps Phokey himself.

The biologists tried to remember Phokey's extraordinary journeys. They drew a map of his travels in the sand.

"Let's see, that's nearly 1,000 miles he's swum! And those are just the trips we know about. What a chase he's led us on!"

The biologists watched Phokey as he swam toward some young sea lions surfing in the breaking waves. He joined them and tried riding a wave too. But he wasn't as skilled a surfer as the sea lions. The otter tumbled over and over as the big wave crashed onto the shore and dumped him on the beach. He lay very still for a minute.

"He won't be trying that again!" said one of the biologists, as the retreating surf dragged Phokey back into the water. But without wasting a minute, the otter caught another wave and rode it toward shore. This time he peeled out of the wave with a professional sea lion twist, just as it crashed onto the beach. Again and again Phokey surfed the waves, until the sea lions left and he dove after them.

As he surfaced for a breath of air, Phokey glanced back at the people on the shore. Then he paddled away. The biologists played hide-and-seek with the otter for a while, but soon lost him among the many coves and rocky inlets. They didn't stop searching, but that was the last the biologists ever saw of Phokey the sea otter. Was he simply eluding them? They almost hoped so.

14
Phokey's Secret Island

And yet that was not the last that *anyone* saw of Phokey. One day, an otter and a silvery black-spotted seal were playing in the glistening kelp beds surrounding an island. But it wasn't San Clemente Island.

The otter stretched his long neck high out of the water and looked toward the land. Someone was watching him from the island beach. The person was small and had long, dark hair that gleamed in the sun. She was smiling happily. It was the Chumash fisherman's granddaughter.

"Hello, Phokey. Remember me?" the girl said gently. "Don't worry little otter. I won't tell that you're here. It's a secret between you and me and the seals."

Phokey and the silver seal swam closer to the black-haired girl. They both stared at her curiously.

"Grandfather and I heard that you swam all the way to Coronados Islands, south of the Mexican border! Those biologists said it must have been you, because someone told them an otter was swimming with the seals there. It was you, wasn't it?"

47

Phokey climbed on top of his floating silver friend so that he had a better view of the talking girl. The seal made a nice plump raft, until it started sinking. Phokey heard the girl laughing.

"Someday, maybe many sea otters will live in the islands once again. Like you did long ago when my people lived here."

The black-haired girl looked down and smiled. In her hands she held some treasures she had found on the beach: a small, pearly abalone, the delicate violet shell of a sea urchin, and Phokey's old green and white tags. They were worn but she could just make out the numbers.

"You can stay here as long as you like. Play with your seal friends. You're free!"

The silver seal splashed Phokey with its flippers and sank under the water. Beams of golden sunlight streamed through the lush forest of kelp. It looked like an underwater cathedral.

"It's so beautiful under the sea," whispered the girl with a smile. "What a lucky sea otter you are."

With a flip of his tail, Phokey dove after the seal, and the two vanished beneath the glassy surface of the ocean. But the girl could still see through the crystal-clear water, and she watched them playing among the swaying kelp plants in their secret island home.

FUN FACTS ABOUT SEA OTTERS

How Long Do Sea Otters Live?

Wild female sea otters live as long as 15 to 20 years. Males live about 10 to 15 years. Most females give birth for the first time when they are three or four years old. Male otters can't hold territories and breed until they are more than six or seven years old.

White-headed Otters

As a sea otter grows older, its fur often loses color, just as our grandparents' hair turns white. Older otters may have snow-white heads and chests. But younger otters sometimes have light blond heads, too.

What Eats Sea Otters?

In California great white sharks attack sea otters. The sharks probably mistake otters for seals — the sharks' favorite food. In Alaska, bald eagles swoop down and carry away otter pups that are floating on the surface while their mothers are diving for food. When otters come ashore to rest, they may be captured by coyotes in Alaska and hungry brown bears in Russia.

Seeing Underwater and at Night

When you open your eyes underwater, your vision is blurry. But a sea otter can see clearly both underwater and on land. At night, otters can see much better than we can. Inside their eyes is a special layer of tiny crystals that gather and reflect light, causing the otters' eyes to glow in the dark just as a cat's eyes do.

The Warmest Fur in the World

How do sea otters stay warm in the chilly ocean water? They don't have a thick layer of blubber, or fat, like whales and seals do. Instead, otters depend on their thick, water-resistant fur coat to keep them warm and dry. One square inch of sea otter fur contains up to one million hairs!

Good Groomers

Sea otters constantly lick and rub their fur to keep it clean and dry, trapping tiny air bubbles within the underfur. This layer of air helps the otter float as well as stay dry in its cold and wet home.

Always Eating

Sea otters also keep warm by eating a lot. By rapidly burning calories—the fuel from food—the otter creates heat inside its body. Each day a wild otter must eat an amount of food equal to ¼ to ⅓ of its entire body weight to survive. This means that Phokey, who weighed 62 pounds, had to find and eat about 15 to 20 pounds of food every day, worth about 7,500 calories!

Mammals in the Sea

Sea otters are mammals like us. Both otters and people are warm-blooded, breathe air, and make milk to nurse their babies. Because sea otters spend their lives in the ocean, they belong to a special group of mammals known as marine mammals. Seals, whales, and dolphins are also marine mammals.

Sea Otter Menus

California sea otters eat invertebrate animals, such as crabs, abalone, squid, sea stars, clams, and rock oysters. Otters in Alaska and Russia also eat fish. Because most lobsters live south of the sea otters' range in California, otters don't usually get a chance to eat them, as Phokey did.

Favorite Foods

Each California otter has its own unique diet. Most eat only two or three kinds of food. Mothers seem to pass their food preferences on to their pups.

Friends of the Kelp Forest

By eating animals that eat kelp plants, such as sea urchins, sea otters help the kelp forests grow and flourish. In turn, kelp forests provide shelter and food for many different kinds of animals and plants.

Purple Teeth

Some otters eat so many purple-spined sea urchins that their teeth turn lavender! The urchins contain a pigment that stains teeth.

What Was the Strangest Food an Otter Ever Ate?

Seabirds! A few otters in California learned to capture and eat western grebes, cormorants, surf scoters, common loons, and sea gulls. The otter sneaks up on the floating bird from underwater and grabs it by the feet.

The Tool Users

The sea otter is one of the few animals in the world that uses tools. While floating on the surface, an otter often places a stone on its belly and pounds snails, mussels, and other prey against the rock to break open their hard shells. Otters also use tools underwater to pry loose stubborn abalone or urchins wedged tightly in rocky crevices.

Different Tools for Different Otters

Many otters prefer to use certain kinds of tools and have their own special tool-use style. Besides rocks, otters use empty shells, crab claws, wood, kelp, and bricks as tools. One female otter and her daughter always use a glass bottle tool. Another otter's favorite tool is a heavy, flat cement slab that she uses underwater to pry loose abalone from rocks.

Smart Otter Tricks for Finding Food

Sea otters are resourceful and creative about finding new ways to capture and eat their prey. One clever otter learned to search for aluminum soda pop cans after discovering that tiny octopuses ooze through the pop-top opening and hide inside. Another otter learned to reach into a bucket filled with tasty squid on a boat docked in the harbor—not a good habit! Some sea star-eating otters have even discovered how to fold the sea star's arms together so the sticky inner tube feet stick to each other instead of the otters' fur!

Mothers and Pups

Pups stay with their mothers for about six months. A mother otter shares up to half of all the food she catches with her pup, and she nurses her baby with milk made up of 20% to 25% fat—much richer than the ice cream we eat.

Giving Birth

Each year a female sea otter gives birth to a new pup. She is pregnant for about six months. In California, many pups die soon after birth, but biologists aren't sure why. This high loss of pups may be one reason why the California population is growing so slowly.

Weanling Pups

After pups are weaned, the young females stay in the area where they were raised, but the males leave. They often join all-male bachelor groups.

Otter Rafts

Sea otters usually rest close to shore in groups called "rafts," although sometimes you'll see them sleeping alone or in pairs. Rafts in California are small. But in Alaska hundreds of otters sometimes raft together. Sea otters especially like the kelp beds and often wrap themselves in kelp at the surface so they won't drift away while napping. When mealtime comes, otters leave the raft to feed alone.

Otter Talk

Sea otters communicate with each other using sound, smell, and "body language." An otter entering a raft usually nuzzles and sniffs the other otters. Sea otters make at least ten different kinds of sounds. They coo, grunt, whine, whistle, squeal, whimper, squeak, growl, hiss, and scream.

Mothers and pups often call to each other with ear-splitting screams. They can recognize each other's unique "voiceprint," since each otter has a different-sounding call.

Almost Extinct

Once sea otters flourished in the North Pacific ocean. Perhaps 150,000 to 300,000 otters lived along the shores of Japan, Russia, Alaska, and the entire coast of North America to Mexico. But in the mid-1700s, fur traders began to hunt otters for their beautiful fur. By the early 1900s, sea otters were nearly extinct.

A Slow Comeback

A few otter colonies survived in Alaska and Russia, and from these ancestors the northern otter populations gradually grew and recovered. A small group of otters also escaped extinction in Big Sur, California. But these southern otters grew more slowly, and the "threatened" California population still remains small and fragile.

Oil and Otters Don't Mix

When sticky oil mats an otter's fur coat, the otter can't stay warm, and it soon dies. Many otters also swallow the poisonous oil as they try to groom their soiled fur. The devastating 1989 Exxon Valdez oil spill in Alaska killed hundreds of otters and other sea animals.

The Future of Sea Otters

Sea otters throughout the North Pacific still face threats to their survival from pollution, drowning in fishing nets, heavy boat traffic, shooting, illegal hunting by poachers in Russia, and oil spills.

But many people are working hard to protect sea otters and keep our oceans healthy. What can you do to help the sea otters?

- Protect our coastlines from oil spills.
- Don't litter or pollute the ocean or our beaches.
- Respect and protect sea otters and other marine animals.

THE CHUMASH INDIANS

Like the sea otters, for centuries the Chumash Indians lived along the southern California coast and on four of the Channel Islands: Anacapa, Santa Cruz, San Miguel, and Santa Rosa.

The Chumash were a gentle and happy people whose lives were full of sacred legends and ceremonies. The Chumash people had great respect and care for the natural world. They hunted otters and other marine animals but took only what they needed. Accomplished artists, they made beautiful baskets, beadwork, and shell ornaments.

Today, many of the remaining Chumash people still live along the California coast, where they are trying to preserve their ancient spiritual and cultural traditions.

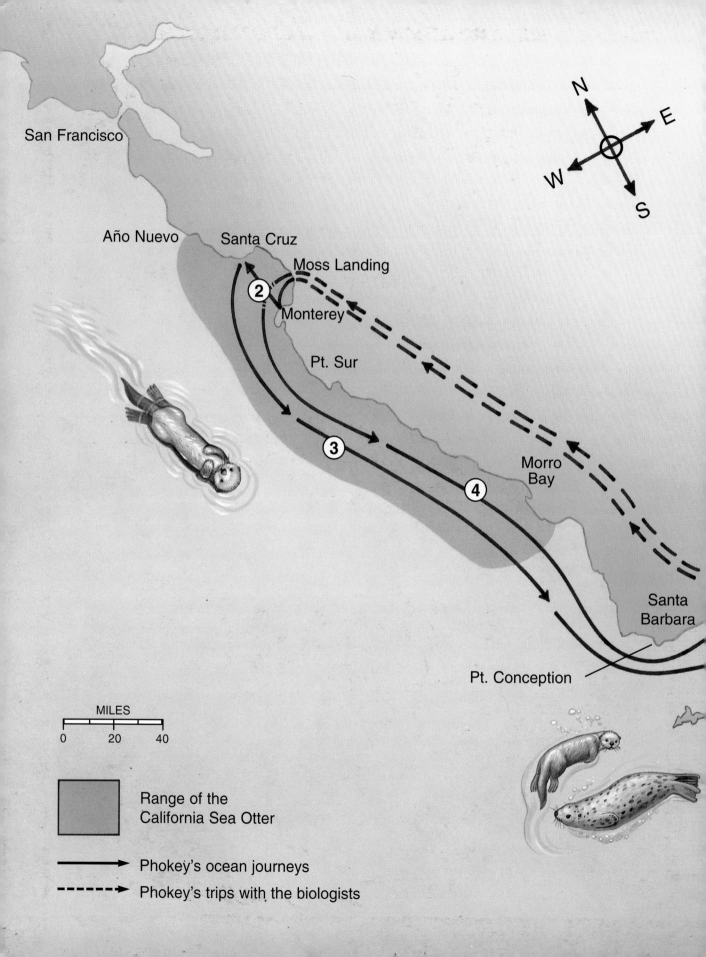

N
E
W
S

San Francisco

Año Nuevo   Santa Cruz
Moss Landing
②
Monterey
Pt. Sur
③
Morro
Bay
④
Santa
Barbara
Pt. Conception

MILES
0   20   40

Range of the
California Sea Otter

→ Phokey's ocean journeys

╌╌→ Phokey's trips with the biologists